The Inuit

by Natalie M. Rosinsky

Content Adviser: Bruce Bernstein, Ph.D.,
Assistant Director for Cultural Resources,
National Museum of the American Indian,
Smithsonian Institution

Reading Adviser: Rosemary G. Palmer, Ph.D.,
Department of Literacy, College of Education
Boise State University

COMPASS POINT BOOKS
MINNEAPOLIS, MINNESOTA

FIRST REPORTS

Compass Point Books
3109 West 50th Street, #115
Minneapolis, MN 55410

Visit Compass Point Books on the Internet at *www.compasspointbooks.com*
or e-mail your request to *custserv@compasspointbooks.com*

On the cover: An Inuit carving

Photographs ©: John Elk III, cover; Charles & Josette Lenars/Corbis, 4; Alison Wright, 7, 14, 32, 36, 39; Library of Congress, 8, 18, 33; Gordon Miller, 9; Doc White/Seapics.com, 10, 28; Staffan Widstrand/Corbis, 11; Wolfgan Kaehler/Corbis, 12–13; Hulton/Archive by Getty Images, 15, 22, 25; David Falconer, 16–17, 40–41; Canadian Museum of Civilization, photographer Vihljalmur Stefansson, negative no. 20288, 19; Reproduced with the permission of the West Baffin Eskimo Cooperative, Cape Dorset, Nunavut, 21, 23, 38; Stapleton Collection/Corbis, 24; Peter Harholdt/Corbis, 26–27; National Archives of Canada/C-124432, 30–31; Geray Sweeney/Corbis, 34–35; Erwin and Peggy Bauer, 37; Reuters/Corbis, 42–43; John Cross/The Free Press, 48.

Creative Director: Terri Foley
Managing Editor: Catherine Neitge
Photo Researcher: Svetlana Zhurkina
Designer/Page production: Bradfordesign, Inc./Les Tranby
Cartographer: XNR Productions, Inc.
Educational Consultant: Diane Smolinski

Library of Congress Cataloging-in-Publication Data
Rosinsky, Natalie M. (Natalie Myra)
    The Inuit / by Natalie M. Rosinsky.
        p. cm. — (First reports)
    Includes bibliographical references and index.
    ISBN 0-7565-0640-9 (hardcover)
    1. Inuit—History. 2. Inuit—Social life and customs. I. Title. II. Series.
    E99.E7R685 2005
    971.9004'9712—dc22   2004000591

Table of Contents

NOTE: In this book, words that are defined in the glossary are
in **bold** the first time they appear in the text.

Who Are the Inuit?

▲ *Inuit girls in Greenland wear brightly colored traditional clothes and sealskin boots.*

The Inuit (pronounced IN-yoo-it) are a native people of the cold Arctic. More than 10,000 years ago, their ancestors crossed a **land bridge** from Asia to North America. These people slowly spread eastward.

The many people who live in the Arctic north

were once known as Eskimos. This word means "eater of raw meat" in one Indian language. It means "snowshoe netter" in another. Today they prefer to be called by their own name, Inuit. A total of about 150,000 Inuit live in northern Russia, the United States, Canada, and Greenland.

An organization called the Inuit **Circumpolar** Conference represents all the Inuit. This group has said that the name Inuit should be used for its people wherever they live. It points out their shared background and way of life.

Yet Inuit in different countries also have their own names for themselves. In Alaska, the people once called Eskimos are the Inupiat and Yupik. In Greenland, they are the Kalaallit. In Russia, they are the Yupik.

Only in Canada do the Inuit people always call themselves Inuit. It means "the people" in one main Inuit language, Inuktitut.

ARCTIC OCEAN

Greenland

Beaufort
Sea
Inuvialuit

Baffin
Bay

Alaska
(U.S.)

Davis Strait

Yukon
Territory

Northwest
Territories

Nunavut

Iqaluit

Nunatsiavut

Labrador
Sea

British
Columbia

C A N A D A

Hudson
Bay

Newfoundland
and
Labrador

0   200   400 miles
0   200   400 kilometers

Alberta

Saskatchewan

Manitoba

Nunavik

Quebec

PACIFIC
OCEAN

Ontario

St. Lawrence River

New
Brunswick

U N I T E D   S T A T E S

N
W   E
S

Inuit lands at time
of European contact

Nunavut Territory

▲ *About 45,000 Inuit live in central and eastern Canada.*

▲ *Mountains ring the Cumberland Sound on Baffin Island near the Arctic Circle.*

Today, about 45,000 Inuit live in central and eastern Canada. While they have much in common with Inuit in other countries, Canada's Inuit have their own history. Some of their **traditions** are gone. Others remain.

Traveling Hunters

▲ *Inuits traveled in large boats called umiaks.*

Crops will not grow in the bitter cold of the far
north. Temperatures there sometimes drop as low as
minus 60 degrees F (minus 51 degrees C). The Inuit
got most of their food from hunting in the sea and on
the land. As the seasons changed, the Inuit traveled

to find and follow food. They expected to move their homes from place to place. They packed their belongings into large boats called umiaks or piled them onto dogsleds.

Seal remains an important food for the Canadian Inuit. Hunters wait patiently until a seal swims up to a breathing hole in the ice. It may be hours or even days before a seal appears. Smart hunters stand where this animal will not smell them or see their shadows.

▲ *An Inuit hunter waits for a seal.*

▲ *An Inuit hunter paddles a small boat called a kayak.*

Whale and walrus are other sea animals the Inuit hunt. One large whale provides as much meat and fat as 1,000 seals. When eaten raw, these foods contain even more vitamins. Tracking down these animals, Inuit hunters once traveled in small boats called **kayaks.** They used spears called **harpoons.**

A fish called **arctic char** remains another important Inuit food. In Canada, hunters still follow the many wild **caribou** that move across the land. Sometimes, Inuit hunt smaller animals such as rabbit and otter. During the brief Arctic summer, Inuit also still gather wild berries.

▲ *Inuits fish for arctic char through a hole in the ice.*

Tools, Clothing, and Shelter

In the past, hunting also provided the Inuit with the materials needed to make tools, clothing, and even shelter. Inuit men used caribou antlers to make harpoons and arrowheads. They built boats covered with walrus hide and sealskin. These materials keep out water. Hunters would sometimes use whale bones for kayak frames, sled runners, and other large tools. Oil made from whale fat was burned for light and heat. Usually, Inuit men were the hunters and builders.

▲ *A lithograph of "The Whale Hunt" by Canadian artist Mary Pudlat*

▲ A baby is carried in the back of a parka called an amaut.

Inuit women were responsible for clothing. To sew, they made needles out of small fish bones. They used **sinews** from caribou or whale for thread. With these tools, Inuit women sewed caribou skin into warm hooded coats called parkas. Special parkas called amauts had pouches in back for carrying babies. Boots, pants, and parkas made from sealskin kept hunters dry at sea. Sometimes, fish skin was also sewn into coats. Soft rabbit fur was used for socks.

Some animal skins had to be made soft before they could be sewn. Women chewed on skins to make them soft. This was an important job because skins were used for clothing, beds, and shelter.

In fall and spring, Inuits built houses of hard earth supported by

▲ An Inuit woman chews animal skin to make it soft enough to sew.

whale bones, stones, or wood. Only in winter or near the North Pole did Inuits carve and stack ice blocks into the round houses called igloos. During the Arctic summer, Inuits often lived in tents made of seal or caribou skin. Softened skins were stretched over wood or whale bone frames. All Inuit homes could quickly be taken apart when hunters needed to move.

▲ *Inuit tents are made with caribou skins.*

Inuit Families

Close families have always been very important to the Inuit. Children lived with their mother and father. Sometimes, a grandmother or grandfather would also live with the family. A mother's and father's relatives were valued equally. Often, these relatives' children might be **adopted** into a

▲ *An Inuit mother and her children in the early 20th century*

family. Children were treasured because they brought joy. They also helped with daily work.

Girls learned to sew, cook, and melt ice for water. Boys learned to hunt and build. Much of their play involved these tasks.

Related families traveled together. In the spring, summer, and fall, this community might have two to

▲ *An entire household could fit on a sled, as shown in this 1915 photo.*

six families. In the winter, the community grew. Twenty-five families might travel together to help one another. Hunters shared the meat they caught with the whole group.

Visiting and storytelling helped pass the time during the long, dark winter. At gatherings, people would sing and dance to walrus skin drums.

Games of skill and contests of strength were other ways to have fun.

There was no formal government or leader. Inuit respected older people for their experience and know-how. They valued good sense.

Often, the oldest, most successful hunter would decide things for a family community. Before making his decisions, he might ask the **shaman** for advice. This person, the Inuit believed, had special knowledge of the spirit world.

The Spirit World

The Inuit believed that spirits exist in all things and creatures. Hunters respected the spirit of each animal they killed. Before butchering a seal, they would offer the dead animal a drink of fresh water. If they did not

▲ *The artwork of Mary Pudlat depicts the spirit of the fish.*

do this, Inuit hunters believed their families would have bad luck. Perhaps a shaman could help them with this or other problems.

The shaman, a respected member of the community, was most often a man. The Inuit believed he had magical powers. A shaman supposedly could cure sickness and tell the future. He supposedly could find lost objects

▲ *An Inuit shaman plays a ceremonial drum.*

and talk with spirits. Inuit believed a shaman could even fly and change himself into an animal!

Special drumming or singing often accompanied this magic. Because they might be evil, shamans were sometimes feared, too.

The Inuit also believed in powerful spirits like gods. The spirit who ruled the ocean was named Sedna. In one story, Sedna created the first whales and seals from her fingers and toes! Breaking any of Sedna's rules or other **taboos** would bring bad luck.

▲ *The spirit Sedna, shown with a spotted bird, ruled the ocean.*

Explorers, Traders, and Whalers

▲ *Martin Frobisher met the Inuit in 1576.*

European explorers traveled to the Arctic hoping to find a short route to China. Englishman Martin Frobisher was the first explorer known to meet the Inuit. His ship arrived in Baffin Island in 1576. Fighting broke out between his sailors and the Inuit. People were killed.

When Frobisher returned to England, he carried off three Inuit. These people later died. Other explorers took an Inuit mother and child captive. They, too, died in Europe.

In 1610, explorer Henry Hudson reached a large bay south of the Arctic Circle, which now bears his name. Fur traders later used his name, too. The Hudson's Bay Trading Company was the Arctic north's biggest trader.

▲ *A 1940s trapper brings furs to the Hudson's Bay Company to trade for money and supplies.*

▲ *An 1878 painting by William Bradford depicts whaling ships in the Arctic.*

For their furs, Inuit received guns, sugar, cloth, and metal tools. There were few other places nearby to trade.

The Hudson's Bay Company became very powerful. Fur trading became and remained an important part of Inuit life for many years.

Between 1719 and 1911, many European and American ships hunted whales in the Arctic. They wanted whale fat for oil and whalebone for ladies' clothes.

▲ The narwhal is a valuable food source for the Inuit. The small whale has a 9 foot (2.7 meter) tusk. Scientists fear the narwhal is becoming scarce.

Sometimes, whalers hired Inuit to work for them. Overall, though, whalers hurt this native people.

Some whalers had diseases that spread to and killed the Inuit. Whalers also did not limit the number of sea animals they killed, which reduced the whale population.

By 1912, parts of the Arctic had few whales left. The Inuit there could no longer get food, clothing, and shelter by hunting whales themselves.

The Inuit also could no longer earn money by hunting whales for others. They could not buy the supplies they wanted. The Inuit had lost important parts of their way of life.

Missionaries at Work

The first Christian **missionaries** came to the Arctic in 1771. During the next 150 years, more arrived. They built missions next to traders' stores. Along with a new religion, missionaries offered the Inuit supplies in hard times.

The missionaries did not accept shamans or some of the other Inuit ways. Yet both Christians and Inuits had a carefully ordered society. Both had rules.

These similar ideas led many Inuit to Christianity.

▲ An 1819 painting shows a missionary meeting with the Inuit.

▲ *Baffin Island signs are written in English and Inuktitut.*

Missionaries wanted the Inuit to know the Bible, but Inuit did not read or write. They spoke all their stories and myths. They learned them by memory. So, missionaries had to create written forms of the Inuit language.

In 19th-century Canada, they used the same system of writing developed earlier for another native group, the Ojibwa. This writing used signs, instead of letters, for the sounds of a language.

A Changed Way of Life

In the 1950s, Canada's Inuit experienced a huge change. The government decided its Inuit people should no longer move from place to place. It forced

▲ *An Inuit man builds a house in 1956. The government forced many Inuit to move to towns.*

them to move into towns. The Canadian government made them live in wood buildings all year long. Sometimes, the government even sent Inuit children far away from their parents. The children lived in schools where only English was spoken and taught.

These decisions were made by people who did not know or respect the Inuit. The government believed these changes would help this native people, but the Inuit themselves believed the government was wrong.

▲ Whale bones mark a
snow-covered grave in Nunavut.

Often, the new towns were far away from good places to hunt. Instead of being independent, the Inuit now needed government supplies just to live.

Some Inuit children no longer knew their people's skills and stories. Sometimes, children did not remember how to talk to their family in their own language. Many Inuit became sad. Some drank too much. Some Inuit killed themselves.

Inuit Art

Canada's government tried to create new jobs for the Inuit in the 1950s. Many of these efforts failed. There was one great success, though. Some government workers helped Inuit people earn money with their art.

▲ *An Inuit carver on Baffin Island*

▲ *An Inuit soapstone carving of a bear*

Small statues of Arctic creatures became very popular. Carved out of soft stone, some figures also showed Inuit people, tales, or myths. Government workers helped Inuit carvers find buyers for these pieces. They also showed the Inuit how to print many copies of their drawings. Soon, Inuit prints became valued around the world.

Some Inuit artists became well known. One famous artist was a woman named Pitseolak Ashoona. She described what her work meant to her. Pitseolak said, "Firstly I did it for the money, but now I hope that when I die I can continue to paint in Heaven."

▲ *"Running with Birds" by Pitseolak Ashoona*

The Inuit Today

Inuit in modern-day Canada govern and do business for themselves. Their independent territory was carved out of Canada. It was created in 1999 and is

▲ *Boats in the bay at Iqaluit, the capital of Nunavut*

called Nunavut, which means "our land" in the Inuktitut language. Inuit also control the regions of Inuvialuit, Nunavik, and Nunatsiavut. Most Canadian Inuit live there, in small towns separated by many miles.

▲ *Inuit schoolchildren build an igloo.*

Inuit run the town councils and work for the governments to which they report.

Inuit today often travel by snowmobile and airplane rather than dogsled and umiak. They watch television,

use computers, wear jeans, and eat pizza.

Yet they also hold on to their past. In the winter, Inuit wear clothing made from the fur of animals, like their ancestors did.

Children learn Inuktitut in school. Some radio and television programs, newspapers, and magazines use this language, too.

Several Inuit organizations keep the traditions alive. Many Inuit still eat food they have hunted. Each spring and summer, towns empty as Inuit families travel to their hunting camps. There, children and teens learn more of the traditional ways.

Unemployment remains a problem for the Inuit. Worldwide laws against seal hunting limit what they earn.

Until recently, Inuit operated small businesses. Now, they plan to start larger ones. These will use arctic land, oil, and creatures in responsible ways.

Such responsibility is part of Inuit tradition. The Inuit look toward a future that includes and respects their past.

▲ During a tour of Canada in 2002, Queen Elizabeth II of England met the people of Nunavut. During a program, they explained how they are keeping their traditions alive.

Glossary

adopted—made someone a member of the family

arctic char—northern freshwater fish; related to trout and salmon

land bridge—land that once joined present-day Alaska and Siberia more than 13,000 years ago; the land that allowed human and animal migration is now beneath the Bering and Chukchi Seas

caribou—a kind of reindeer

circumpolar—the area around Earth's North Pole or South Pole

harpoons—weapons like spears with ropes attached used to hunt seals, walrus, and whales

kayak—a small, narrow fishing boat made out of animal skin

missionaries—people who travel to spread their religion to others

shaman—a healer who is believed to have magical powers or knowledge

sinews—strings of tough flesh

taboos—rules about what should not be done

traditions—a group of people's longtime ways of doing things

Did You Know?

- The most distant object ever seen orbiting the Sun is named after an Inuit goddess. Scientists, who announced the discovery in 2004, named the cold, faraway object Sedna.

- Inuit mix seal fat with berries for a treat similar to ice cream.

- Inuit get vitamin C from eating whale skin.

- Diapers for Inuit babies were made of moss.

At a Glance

Tribal name: Inuit

Divisions worldwide: Inuit in Canada; Inupiat and Yupik in Alaska; Yupik in Russia; Kalaallit in Greenland.

Divisions in Canada: Nunavut Territory; regions of Inuvialuit, Nunavik, and Nunatsiavut.

Past and present locations worldwide: the Arctic, from Siberia through Alaska and Canada to parts of Greenland

Past and present locations in Canada: central and eastern Arctic regions

Traditional houses: igloos, sod houses, and tents

Traditional clothing materials: sealskin, caribou hide

Traditional transportation: dogsleds and boats

Traditional food: seal, arctic char, caribou, whale, walrus, berries

Important Dates

12,000 – 10,000 B.C.	Ancestors of Inuit cross the land bridge from Russia into Alaska.
6000– 4000 B.C.	Ancestors of Inuit spread eastward to Greenland.
A.D.1576	Martin Frobisher is the first European explorer known to visit the Arctic Inuit.
1610	Henry Hudson reaches the bay that is later named for him.
1719– 1911	European whalers hunt in the eastern Arctic.
1771	Christian missionaries in Labrador establish the first Arctic mission.
1800s– 1930s	Fur traders hunt and trap animals in the Arctic.
1870s	Missionaries create written versions of the Inuit language.
1950s	Canadian government forces the Inuit into towns with permanent houses.
1977	Inuit Circumpolar Conference is organized.
1999	Nunavut becomes the first independent Inuit territory within Canada.

Want to Know More?

At the Library

Bierhorst, John, ed. *The Dancing Fox: Arctic Folktales*. New York: William Morrow, 1997.

Finley, Carol. *Art of the Far North: Inuit Sculpture, Drawing, and Printmaking*. Minneapolis: Lerner, 1998.

Tookoome, Simon, with Sheldon Oberman. *The Shaman's Nephew: A Life in the Far North*. Toronto: Stoddart Kids, 1999.

On the Web

For more information on the Inuit, use FactHound to track down Web sites related to this book.

1. Go to *www.facthound.com*
2. Type in a search word related to this book or this book ID: 0756506409.
3. Click on the *Fetch It* button.

Your trusty FactHound will fetch the best Web sites for you!

On the Road

The Canadian Museum of Civilization
100 Laurier St.
Gatineau, Quebec
Canada J8X 4H2
800/555-5621
To see Inuit art, tools, and clothing in the Hall of First Peoples

National Museum of the American Indian on the National Mall
Fourth Street and Independence Avenue Southwest
Washington, DC 20560
202/287-2020
To visit the Smithsonian Institution's new museum dedicated to Native Americans

Index

About the Author

Natalie M. Rosinsky writes about history, social studies, economics, science, and other fun things. One of her two cats usually sits on her computer as she works in Mankato, Minnesota. Natalie earned graduate degrees from the University of Wisconsin and has been a high school and college teacher.